The Bizarre History of Beauty

HORRENDOUS HAIR CARE

ANITA CROY

Gareth Stevens PUBLISHING

Please visit our website, www.garethstevens.com.
For a free color catalog of all our high-quality books,
call toll free 1-800-542-2595 or fax 1-877-542-2596.

Cataloging-in-Publication Data
Names: Croy, Anita.
Title: Horrendous hair care / Anita Croy.
Description: New York : Gareth Stevens Publishing, 2019. | Series: The bizarre history of beauty | Includes glossary and index.
Identifiers: LCCN ISBN 9781538226896 (pbk.) | ISBN 9781538226889 (library bound)
Subjects: LCSH: Hair–Juvenile literature. | Hair–Care and hygiene–Juvenile literature.
Classification: LCC QP88.3 C79 2019 | DDC 646.724–dc23

First Edition

Published in 2019 by
Gareth Stevens Publishing
111 East 14th Street, Suite 349
New York, NY 10003

Produced for Gareth Stevens by Calcium
Editors: Sarah Eason and Tim Cooke
Designers: Clare Webber and Lynne Lennon
Picture researcher: Rachel Blount

Picture credits: Cover: Shutterstock: Dean Bertoncelj; Inside: Library of Congress: p. 32; Shutterstock: Everett Historical: pp. 4, 19b, 27t, 34; HiddenCatch: pp. 1, 42; Rosa Jay: p. 11t; JPC-PROD: p. 15b; Evgeny Kabardin: p. 41t; Kdonmuang: p. 41b; Merrymuuu: p. 43t; Photographee.eu: p. 40; Photolinc: p. 17t; Kristin Smith: p. 37; Victorian Traditions: p. 25b; Mahathir Mohd Yasin: p. 43b; Wikimedia Commons: pp. 13, 17b, 35b; Anagoria: p. 9b; Guillaume Blanchard: p. 8; Mathew Brady: p. 27b; Louis Calvete: p. 28, 31b; CeStu: p. 5t; Cornelis Jonson van Ceulen: p. 19t; Sir Anthony Van Dyck: p. 18; José Echenagusia Errazquin: p. 7b; Roger Fenton: p. 26; Unknown, probably Jean-Baptiste André Gautier-Dagoty: p. 21t; 1863: excavated by Léon Heuzey and Henri Daumet: p. 10; Jebulon: p. 7t; Nicolas de Largillière: p. 22; Nicolas de Larmessin: p. 20; Albert Lynch: p. 14; Maarjaara: p. 6; MGM: p. 30; After Pierre Mignard: p. 21b; Naval History & Heritage Command: p. 29t; Jac. de Nijs/Anefo; Restoration by User:Adam Cuerden: p. 33; Fred C. Palmer: p. 29b; Ashley Pomeroy: p. 35t; Purchased in 1811 from Rondanini Palace: p. 11b; Rauantiques: p. 24; Tim Schapker: p. 39; Joseph Karl Stieler: p. 25t; Titian: p. 16; U.S. National Archives and Records Administration: pp. 21t, 36; United Press International, photographer unknown: p. 38; Walters Art Museum: p. 9t; Wellcome Images: p. 23; Workshop of Rogier van der Weyden: p. 12; Wonderlane: p. 5b; Francisco de Zurbarán: p. 15t.

Printed in the United States of America

CPSIA compliance information: Batch #CS18GS:
For further information contact Gareth Stevens, New York, New York at 1-800-542-2595.

-CONTENTS-

Chapter 1

ANCIENT -HAIR-

For a long time, hair has been associated with attractiveness and power. Over the centuries, different styles and colors have come in and out of fashion.

Around 1500 BC, the Assyrians ruled Babylonia in the Middle East. Their skill at dyeing, curling, and layering their hair made them the leading hairstylists in the region.

GET CURLING!

For the Assyrians, hairstyles gave them status. It was not just hair that was styled in Babylon. Beards were also oiled, tinted, and perfumed. As a sign of just how important they were, Assyrian women sometimes wore false beards during meetings. Fashionable Assyrian hair and beard styles included the **symmetrical cut**. People curled their hair and beards by wrapping it around iron bars that were heated red-hot in a fire. They sometimes set their hair on fire!

Assyrian men curled their hair and beards into elaborate designs.

THAT'S MY COLOR

Before they were conquered by the Assyrians, Babylonian men liked to show their power by dusting their long, flowing locks with gold dust. The emperors of Persia, in what is now Iran, laced their beards with gold thread. Gold made them feel more powerful. The ancient Egyptians loved colored hair. The wigs and **hair extensions** they often wore were blue, green, blonde, and gold.

This stone carving shows the head of a Celtic warrior. These warriors dyed their hair blue and went into battle naked to terrify their enemies.

It was the ancient Greeks who first thought that blondes had more fun. In the Greek world, the lighter the hair, the better. The Romans who conquered Greece in the second century BC copied Greek styles. They lightened their hair using wood ash and various **minerals**. When darker colors were in, copper filings, oak apples, and a mixture of blood-sucking **leeches** soaked in wine and vinegar did the job—as long as the gunk did not slide straight off your head!

The long-haired, long-beared Merovingians, who lived in what is now France between the sixth and eighth centuries AD, believed their strength came from their red hair. Meanwhile, the Celts dyed their hair blue using a plant called wood. They thought it frightened their enemies.

For Greek women, light hair echoed the hair of the gods.

THE POWER
- OF HAIR -

More than any other part of the body, hair has a special status. Some of the best-known myths and legends over the centuries have given hair a starring role.

The popular fairy tale of Rapunzel is based on an Iranian myth over 3,000 years old. In the story, Rapunzel is imprisoned in a tower. She grows her hair so long she can lower it to allow a prince to climb up and release her. They fall in love and are married.

The Greek god Apollo was often potrayed wearing a **laurel** crown around his head.

LEAVE MY HAIR ALONE!

Rapunzel's story reflects the power often associated with hair. Throughout history, some warriors scalped their victims, cutting the skin and hair from their heads. The Manchu rulers of China forced their subjects to shave off all but a single long piece of hair as a sign of submission. Meanwhile, slaves everywhere often had their hair shaved off to show their low status in society.

IT'S ALL GREEK TO ME

In one Greek myth, the priestess Medusa was famed for her beauty and her gorgeous cascading hair. The goddess Athena was so jealous that she turned Medusa's flowing locks into a head of writhing snakes. Any man who looked at Medusa was turned to stone.

In ancient Rome, Emperor Julius Caesar covered his balding head with a crown made from laurel leaves. He was copying the Greeks, who awarded laurel crowns to athletes who won events in the Olympic Games. Thanks to Caesar, the laurel crown became a symbol of **nobility** in Rome. It was worn by wealthy Romans even if they had hair.

Medusa was finally killed by the Greek hero Perseus, son of the god Zeus.

hello beautiful

In the Bible, Samson was an Israelite warrior with long, flowing hair that gave him huge strength. He fell in love with Delilah. She was paid by Samson's enemies to discover the secret of his great strength. She kept asking him until eventually he told her. One night, she chopped off his hair while he slept. When he awoke, all his strength was gone.

When Delilah cut Samson's hair, he lost all his formidable strength.

FALSE
- HAIR -

The ancient Egyptians knew a thing or two about hair. They believed hair was sacred, so they cut off their own hair and wore wigs instead!

In Egypt's hot climate, most people shaved their heads or kept their hair short to avoid sweating. They did not wash their hair often, because they believed it would disturb the spirit who looked after the head. A wig was cooler to wear and easier to keep clean.

IT'S HOT IN HAIR!

The richest Egyptians wore wigs made from real hair. Most people wore wigs of wool, palm fibers, or straw to protect their heads from the sun. Some people put a cake of perfumed wax on top of the wig. The wax melted and kept the wearer cool. Egyptians used wet mud or a jelly made from **quince** soaked in water to set their hair.

Egyptian wigs had the effect of making everyone look very similar!

CHANGING STYLES

Egyptian wigs started out small and curled, but over centuries they became more elaborate. Some large wigs had long sides that fell down to the wearer's chest. Later wigs went for maximum bling, with lots of **braids** woven around gold tubes and sprinkled with real gold powders. For men, the look was often completed with a fake beard—and even some powerful women wore fake beards. To demonstrate their power, **pharaohs** liked their fake beards to be made from solid gold.

An Egyptian woman with hair down over her shoulders plays an instrument called a sistrum.

hello beautiful

Queen Hatshepsut ruled Egypt in the fifteenth century BC. She was only the second female pharaoh. As a sign of her power, all official statues of the queen showed her with a fake gold beard, just like the male pharaohs. The beard may have helped her image. Hatshepsut was one of the most successful of all the pharaohs, ruling for 20 years.

Hatshepsut expanded Egyptian trade and commissioned many new buildings.

THE CLASSICAL
- WORLD -

The Greeks favored the natural look when it came to their hair. The Romans, as usual, mixed and matched trends from both Egypt and Greece.

Before the fifth century BC, Greek women put fresh flowers in their hair and wore it long. Later, they began pulling their hair back into a knot or coil at the back, called a chignon.

Two Greek women pick flowers with their hair tied up behind their heads in hairnets.

AU NATUREL

The most fashionable hair was blonde, following a trend set by the Greek goddesses, who were depicted with light-colored hair. Women who could afford it achieved a yellow hue by sprinkling gold or **saffron** powder in their hair. Women who were less well off lightened their hair with a mixture of **potash** water and yellow flowers. The Romans copied some Greek fashions, but overall they preferred the complex hair designs they knew from Queen Cleopatra and other prominent Egyptians. Romans who did not have a slave to fix their hairstyles had them styled in a public hair salon.

KEEP YOUR HAIR ON

Baldness was not a good look in Greece and Rome. In Greece, a popular potion to restore the hair included rose essence, wine, and olive oil. Another was a blend of cumin, pigeon droppings, crushed horseradish, and nettles. Failing that, men simply smeared their heads with pigeon droppings or goat's urine. The Romans had all kinds of baldness remedies. When the emperor Julius Caesar's hair started to fall out, his lover Queen Cleopatra suggested he apply a paste of bear grease, deer marrow, horses' teeth, and ground-up mice. When that failed, he gave up and started wearing his laurel crown.

The Greek philosopher Aristotle tried goat's urine as a cure for baldness.

to die for

Hair fashions changed quickly in ancient Rome—even for statues. When Roman women had their portraits sculpted, they got the sculptor to create removable hair. That allowed them easily to replace old styles with the latest fashion. Hairstyles changed so often that historians use the hair in statues and paintings as a handy way to identify periods in Roman history.

Even Roman statues had the lastest hairstyles—no matter how unflattering!

Chapter 2

THE MIDDLE - AGES -

During the Middle Ages, hair revealed a lot about a person, including their position in society, whether they were married, and even their religious beliefs.

Hair was a low priority for medieval women. For much of the Middle Ages, the idea of beauty was based on having as high a forehead as possible. Women achieved the effect by plucking their eyebrows and pushing back their hair so it could barely be seen.

This portrait shows Isabella of Portugal in around 1450 with her hair pushed back.

COVER UP

In the early Middle Ages, wealthy women wore their hair loose or in two long **plaits** on either side of the head. Married women wore their hair tied back in a chignon covered with fabric or a woven net. Some women plaited their hair and coiled it above their ears.

As the Middle Ages went on, there was a new focus on **modesty**. Christianity, Islam, and Judaism all condemned long hair as encouraging **immoral** behavior.

Women achieved both a modest appearance and a high forehead by concealing their hair with a hat, hood, or **veil**. One popular medieval style was a very tall conical hat with a veil at the front.

This piece of art shows Russian priests with beards and long hair. Later, Christian priests turned against the fashion.

WHAT ABOUT MEN?

Until the fifteenth century, the Catholic Church set the rules on personal grooming—including how long men's hair should be, whether or not they wore beards, and acceptable hair coverings for women. The church said that hair should be short, so servants and the poor all wore their hair short. Although more important men often had slightly longer hair, even monarchs had to obey the rules. In the ninth century, the French King Louis II followed church teaching and had his long hair cut as short as a monk's. In 1073, Pope Gregory banned beards among the clergy, and soon everyone stopped growing beards. In 1096, the Archbishop of Rouen in France announced that any man with a beard would be expelled from the church! Even in the twelfth century, King Henry I of England was forced to cut his hair and shave off his beard after a priest delivered a strong sermon against long hair and beards.

DO IT
- YOURSELF -

Medieval barbers often doubled as doctors. They removed patients' blood and set bones, as well as shaving beards. They did not have time to cut hair, too!

Joan of Arc became a national heroine when she led French soldiers into battle against an English army.

Most people cut their own hair. It was quite easy to keep up with trends, because they moved slowly. The bowl-shaped pageboy cut for men lasted from the eleventh to the sixteenth century. It might have been so popular because it was so easy to do: people simply placed a bowl over the head and cut off any exposed hair.

EARLY TRENDS

One of the first women to have a pageboy haircut was the fifteenth-century French soldier Joan of Arc. It only became a trend for women around 500 years later, in the early twentieth century. Monks' hairstyles changed even slower. From the eighth century, a monk's hair was shaved off except for a circular strip around the head. This style was called a tonsure. It was a sign that the monk had renounced worldly fashions.

HAIR TREATMENTS

Women's hair might have been hidden under hats and veils, but they still wanted it to look good. There were all kinds of home recipes for hair products, including a potion made by boiling a lizard in olive oil. Egg whites gave the hair body and structure, while nettles mixed in vinegar cured dry scalps. A mixture of vinegar, berry juice, broom, and sage got rid of bugs called lice. Bear fat was said to increase hair growth and lanolin was a popular conditioner. It was made from the oil trapped in sheep's wool, as well as flax seeds and hemp oil.

A monk's tonsure was a sign that he was more interested in spiritual things than in looking good.

to die for

Hair dyeing was in—and it took a while! For blonde hair, people boiled walnut shells and bark, added flowers, and put the liquid on their hair. They covered the hair with leaves and left it for two days. Then they added henna, dust from crocus flowers, and other ingredients and left it all for another three days. After all that, at least the color was said to last!

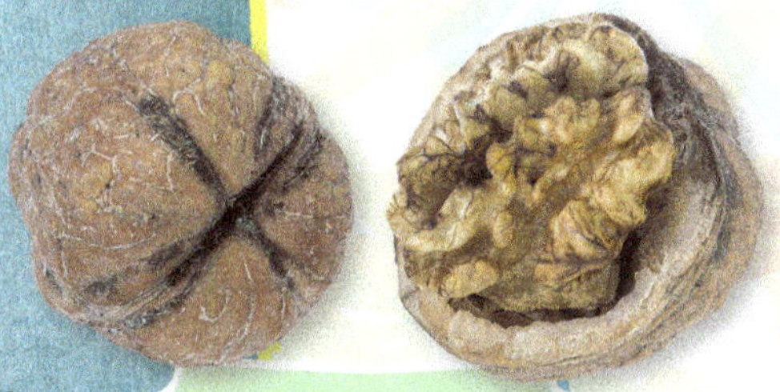

Walnut shells are still used as a source of dye today.

Chapter 3

THE EARLY -MODERN WORLD-

As Europe left the Dark Ages behind, hairstyles became more showy. In the sixteenth century, an English queen changed how people wore their hair.

In this painting of Mary and Jesus, the artist Titian painted Mary with the red hair fashionable in Venice, where he lived.

At the end of the Middle Ages, women still wore their hair under caps to please the Catholic Church. These caps were anything but modest, however. Made from fabrics such as velvet and covered with jewels and ribbons, the most glamorous caps came from Milan in Italy. They were only worn by the most fashionable women.

HIDING AWAY

Although the church disapproved, the fashion for colored hair was so popular that some women reached for their homemade dyes. A popular dye for blonde hair used henna, gorse flowers, saffron, eggs, and calf kidneys. In sixteenth-century Venice, women achieved a fashionable copper red color by putting **caustic soda** on their hair and then sitting in bright sunlight.

Eggs were a standard ingredient in recipes for creating yellow hair.

Women who wanted their hair to be jet black achieved the effect by using combs made of lead. However, the poisonous lead caused some women to suffer kidney failure.

RED-HAIRED QUEEN

Queen Elizabeth I ruled from 1558 to 1603. During that time, England not only ruled the world—it also set the hair fashions of the day. Elizabeth's red hair meant that red hair became a must for English nobles. Men dyed their hair and beards red to show their loyalty to the queen. Women dyed their hair, too, but they used a dye that contained sulfur and lead, which are both **toxic**. The poisons caused sickness, headaches, and nosebleeds.

When she became an older woman, Queen Elizabeth I usually wore a wig with short, curled red hair.

When Elizabeth's hair thinned, she began wearing wigs. She owned more than 80 wigs in a range of styles, all made from expensive imported hair. No one else could afford so many wigs—but at least wearing wigs did not make them sick. In 1587, Elizabeth had her cousin, Mary Queen of Scots, beheaded for trying to seize the throne. As Mary's head fell to the ground, her **auburn**-haired wig also fell off, revealing her real hair, which was short and gray.

WAR OF THE -HAIRSTYLES-

Who would have thought that two contrasting hairstyles could get caught up in a war? That is just what happened during the English Civil War in the seventeenth century.

Charles I became king of England in 1625. He and his followers had long, curly hair or wigs topped with elaborate hats or ostrich feathers. Their clothes were just as ornate, with ribbons, lace, and jewels.

THE KINGS

For many people in England, the appearance of these so-called Cavaliers showed that they were **vain** and interested only in pleasure. Charles's political opponents, called Puritans, looked very different.

This triple portrait shows King Charles I in 1636, giving a clear view of the long, curled hair that his opponents disliked so much.

They cut their hair short and refused to wear wigs as a sign of their loyalty to the Protestant branch of Christianity. They wore plain, dark clothes, in contrast to the flamboyant clothes Cavaliers wore.

The Puritans believed in a sense of duty and hard work, and rejected excessive luxury and pleasure.

CIVIL WAR

The appearances of the two groups reflected very different ideas about politics. In 1642, the difference led to civil war. In 1649, Charles paid for opposing the Puritans by having his head cut off. Just before he died, he asked the executioner, "Is my hair well?" The Puritans set up their own government, which lasted from 1653 until 1658. Life was not much fun under the Puritans. There was lots of hard work and prayer—and no glamorous hair.

to die for

The Puritans had strong views on how hair should be worn. For men it had to be short, off the face, and definitely uncurled. The Cavaliers called the Puritans "Roundheads" because of the shape of their hair (remember the bowl look?). Women could have long hair—but it had to be hidden underneath a plain white cap.

A Puritan family with plain clothes and simple hairstyles share a meal in a home without any decoration.

BIG
- HAIR -

France's Sun King, Louis XIV, began an era of excess in fashion, with towering wigs and extravagant decoration.

The fashions in France could hardly have been more different from the modest Puritan styles of England. At Louis's court at Versailles, "more" was always better. During his long reign from 1643 to 1715, Louis increasingly wore wigs. Not only did they make him look taller—they also hid his bald head. Louis's male courtiers followed, wearing wigs with curls cascading below the shoulders and a bang, or fringe, across the forehead.

Madame de Fontanges is said to have created a hairdressing sensation—by accident.

FRANCE RULES

In contrast, women's hair seemed quite restrained. The fashionable look was to pin the hair up, leaving just one tumbling lock free. Then Madame de Fontanges, one of the king's favorite companions, set a new fashion when she lost her hat out hunting. She piled her hair into a loose knot on top of her head and secured it with a lace-edged garter. Louis approved and the "fontange" was born. It stayed in fashion for the next three centuries.

PILE IT HIGH

By the late eighteenth century, women wore their hair in piles up to 3 feet (0.9 m) tall. The hair was supported by horsehair pads and stiffened with a paste of flour and water. Courtiers competed to decorate their hair. One woman had a model of her son's nursery in her hair, while another had a ship in full sail. This tall hair gave its wearers headaches, sore necks, and little sleep. In addition, it took so long to create the styles that they were only done once a month. The unwashed, floured hair became infested with **vermin**. Women cut slits in the stiffened walls of hair to let head lice escape.

Women added extensions to their natural hair.

hello beautiful

Louis XIV set hair trends across Europe. When his hair started to thin, he employed 48 wigmakers to keep him supplied with wigs to hide his early baldness. Once the king started wearing a wig, even courtiers with plenty of hair followed. The fashion for wigs took off not just at Versailles, but also across Europe.

Once Louis XIV took to wearing wigs, everyone followed suit.

WORLD OF
- THE WIG -

It would take a revolution to stop the French from wearing their wigs. But they continued to be popular in England until the next century.

In France, expensive wigs were a status symbol for most of the eighteenth century. Then, in 1789, the French overthrew their king and the nobility in a revolution. Overnight, wearing fancy wigs was out of fashion.

BIG WIGS

In Britain, in contrast, wigs remained a sign of social status. Anyone who could afford a wig wore one. People who could not afford to buy a wig styled their hair so it looked like a wig! In colonial America, meanwhile, wigs were associated with the colonies' British rulers. On the eve of the American Revolution (1765–1783), Benjamin Franklin opposed the wearing of wigs as a sign of opposition to British rule in America.

The best wigs were so expensive people left them to their families in their wills.

A PUFF OF POWDER

In the late eighteenth century, it became fashionable to powder wigs with **starch**. The powder was thrown into the air so it settled on the wig. Wealthy people had a special room just for powdering wigs, or wore special dressing gowns and put a paper cone over their faces to avoid getting covered in the powder. Women preferred pastel shades of powder, such as pink and violet, while men went for white or gray. Poor people dusted their wigs with flour. Getting caught in the rain ruined a powdered wig. Wigs also had a habit of bursting into flames if a wearer sat too close to the fire.

A barber powders a wig supported on a special wig stand.

to die for

In 1798, British Prime Minister William Pitt introduced a tax on wig powder. One estimate is that people at the time were using enough flour and starch on their wigs to make bread for 50,000 people, so Pitt saw a chance to raise money. However, his tax was so unpopular that people stopped using powder on their wigs—and soon stopped wearing wigs, too.

Chapter 4

THE NINETEENTH - CENTURY -

As the nineteenth century dawned, the impact of the French Revolution was still being felt. Natural hair was back in fashion and wigs were a thing of the past.

Early in the century, the Empress Josephine, wife of the French Emperor Napoleon, set the fashions. Women copied Josephine's hairdo, which was inspired by ancient Greece. The hair was curled at the front and gathered into a chignon at the back, with minimal ornament.

Empress Josephine started what was called the Empire look, based on ancient Greek styles.

MALE MODELS

For men, the model was the English **dandy** Beau Brummell. Brummell was said to employ three hairdressers—one to cut the back of his hair, one to cut the right side, and one to cut the left—all at the same time. With his long, curled hair, he looked like a **Romantic** poet. The Romantic artistic movement praised long hair as being natural and wild. The days of the wig were gone.

VICTORIAN ERA

In 1837, Victoria was crowned queen of Great Britain. For the next 60 years she dictated hair fashion in Britain and Europe. The queen favored a modest appearance. Her hair was natural, but she concealed it under a **bonnet** or a cap. Ladies were considered undressed if they left home without a bonnet. Women never cut their hair. Although young girls were allowed to wear their hair long, married women had to put their hair up and keep it hidden.

In Victorian England, a modest appearance was a sign of good behavior. The Victorians believed that a woman's hair revealed her personality: curly-haired women were thought to be sweeter and kinder than women with straight hair. Women who dared to show off their long hair were considered shocking. Such daring women were often associated with **bohemian** artistic movements or were actresses in the theater.

The Romantic composer Ludwig van Beethoven had wild, flowing hair.

Even late in the nineteenth century, women kept their hair hidden beneath bonnets.

WATCH THOSE - WHISKERS! -

In the middle of the nineteenth century, men went beard and mustache crazy. Following the lead of military heroes of the day, clean-shaven faces were out of fashion.

British soldiers grew facial hair in the Crimean War as a defense against the bitterly cold winters.

The military were to thank for the nineteenth century craze for facial hair. With the exception of Bavarian soldiers, who were banned from growing facial hair, soldiers across Europe sported mustaches and beards.

KEEPING WARM

The elegant whiskers of earlier centuries were replaced by huge, bushy beards and long whiskers that left just enough room to reveal the mouth. The Crimean War (1854–1856), when British soldiers fought Russians in the Crimea, was the inspiration for this bushy look. The freezing winter temperatures and a lack of shaving soap led the British army to lift its ban on beards. Full facial hair was one way of keeping warm—and it was free!

OUR AMERICAN COUSIN

In the United States, it did not take much for men to abandon shaving, which was still tricky and unsafe. The market was flooded with equipment, including a portable heated curler to curl the mustache ends. The mustache cup had a raised lip-guard to keep drinks from touching the hair. In 1861, the character Lord Dundreary in a popular play sported magnificent side-whiskers. These whiskers, known as "dundrearies," became popular in both Britain and the United States. By coincidence, Abraham Lincoln, the first U.S. president with a beard, was watching the same play—*Our American Cousin*—when he was assassinated in 1865.

A nineteenth-century German businessman in London sports a distinctive forked beard.

hello beautiful

During the Civil War (1861–1865), Union Major General Ambrose Burnside (right) sported a distinctive mustache and whiskers with a clean-shaven chin. He created a new fashion for unbroken bushy facial hair, named "burnsides" for him. The two parts of the name were later reversed to give the style the name "sideburns," which is still used today.

GIVE US - A WAVE -

When the curling tong appeared near the end of the nineteenth century, it was not as modern as it seemed. In fact, it was more than 5,000 years old!

In 1872, Marcel Grateau opened a hairdressing salon in Paris, France. As a teenager, Grateau had worked grooming horses. He put that training to good use!

CURL, BABY, CURL

The ancient Babylonians had learned to curl the hair by wrapping it around hot iron rods. Grateau used a heated curling iron to make tight, frizzy waves that sat close to his clients' heads. In a rush one day, he used the curling iron upside down—and created a new craze. Soon called the Marcel wave, it looked more natural than the earlier tight curls. It also worked equally well on curly and straight hair. Grateau patented his curling tong in 1890, and the style spread. The Marcel wave would stay in fashion for the next 50 years.

In the early twentieth century, waved hairstyles became more elaborate.

to die for

Curling tongs had been making waves since the Babylonians, but before Grateau invented electric tongs, they could be lethal. The tongs were heated in fires, so there was no way to regulate how hot they got. Women paid the price of scalp burns and singed hair to get their hair curled just right.

Electric curling tongs gave women control over how hot they became.

CROWNING GLORY

Even before Grateau's innovation, hair had become big business. Nineteenth-century magazines devoted many words to instructing women just how to get the right "look." They advised washing the hair once a month and gave precise details of how to dry and style the hair using curling tongs. It was a slow process because women had a lot of hair. To make the wave last longer, women rubbed **macassar oil** into their hair. The palm-based oil had become popular with men earlier in the century to give their hair a slicked-back look. The oil was so greasy that Victorian chairs had special macassar covers to keep it from seeping into the cloth.

Victorian men achieved the typical slicked-back appearance by using macassar oil.

Chapter 5

THE TWENTIETH CENTURY

In the twentieth century, hairstyles came in and went out of fashion with dizzying speed. Meanwhile, the choice of hair products had never been greater.

In the first half of the century, movie stars became trendsetters for all types of fashion, including hairstyles. Women watched their idols on the big screen and wanted to copy their look.

I'M A STAR

In 1931, the movie star Jean Harlow bleached her hair **platinum** using dime-store coloring. She made hair dyeing acceptable overnight. During World War II (1939–1945), authorities asked the actress Veronica Lake to change her hairstyle. Female factory workers who copied her long hair kept getting caught in machinery! Hair in the 1950s was styled and **bouffant**, but in the late 1960s it became longer and more natural. In the 1970s, millions of women copied Farrah Fawcett's feathered blonde hair

Veronica Lake often wore her thick, long hair over one eye.

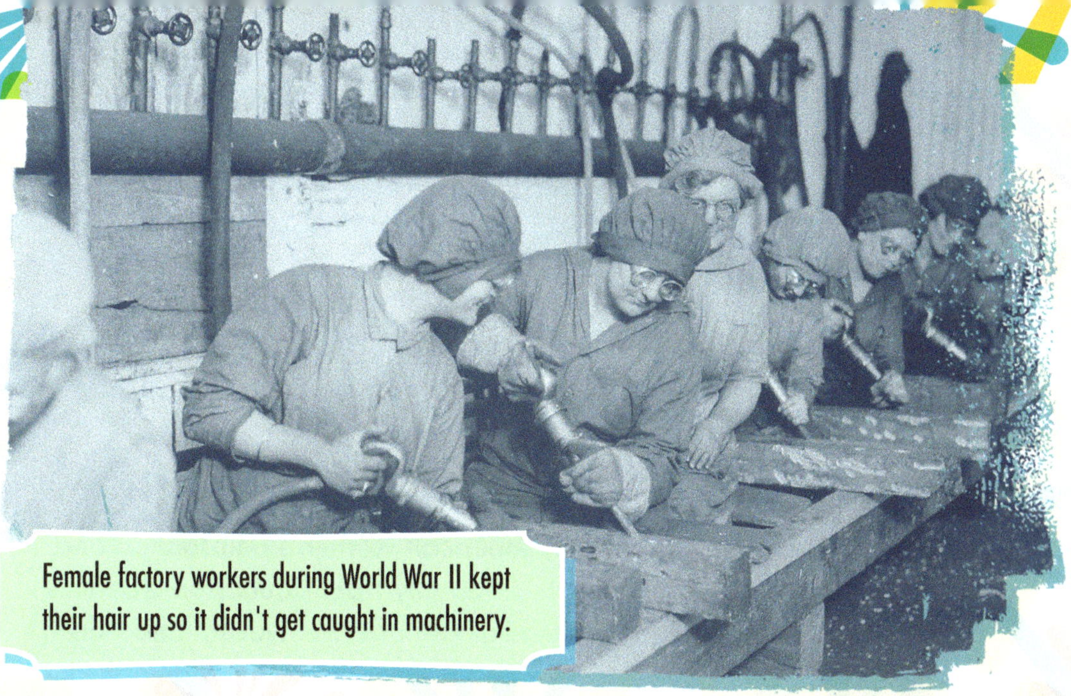

Female factory workers during World War II kept their hair up so it didn't get caught in machinery.

in the TV show *Charlie's Angels*. Two decades later, everyone wanted Jennifer Aniston's haircut in the hit TV show *Friends*. It wasn't only actresses who set trends. In the1990s, Britain's glamorous Princess Diana launched many different hairstyles.

A MAN'S WORLD

Men's hair also went through decades of change thanks to the movie and music industries. Men started the century slicking back their hair and sporting handlebar mustaches. In the 1930s, movie star Clark Gable's pencil mustache was the look to copy. When Elvis Presley burst onto the music scene in the 1950s, men copied his combed-back hair and bushy sideburns. The mop tops of the Beatles set the trend in the 1960s, as did the long-haired, bearded hippies in the 1970s. In the 1990s, the **grunge** movement saw young men with long, matted hair like the singer Kurt Cobain.

This machine was built in 1923 to style the hair in a "permanent wave," or perm.

AFRICAN AMERICAN
-HAIR-

Early in the twentieth century, two African American businesswomen revolutionized hair care for black women in the United States.

In the early twentieth century, many black women tried to straighten their hair in order to style it.

African American women's hair looked and grew differently from Caucasian women's hair. For centuries, however, it had been treated largely the same. Many black Americans lacked the resources to pay for their own hair-care products.

BIG BUSINESS

Two women from slave families changed things for millions of other African American women. Annie Turnbo Malone set up a business selling hair straighteners and oils for black women in Illinois. In 1902, she moved her business to St. Louis. One of Malone's sales agents was Sarah Breedlove. In 1905, a recipe for hair oil came to Breedlove in a dream. It became the basis of her own hair-care business, under the name Madam C. J. Walker. Walker became one of the first self-made women millionaires in America. She sold shampoos and conditioning products just for African Americans, and employed black women in her factories.

Malone and Walker created a new market of specialty hair products. They invented hair irons and oils to straighten naturally curly African hair.

The "Afro" became a political statement for black women and men in the 1960s and 1970s.

NOT SO STRAIGHT

Later in the century, some African American women rejected the idea of straightening their hair to make it resemble white women's hair. Some saw this as a denial of their heritage. In the 1960s, some of them started to leave their hair in its natural "**Afro**" state as part of the **Black Pride** movement. They were making a political statement that they were proud of their African American heritage and would no longer accept white standards of beauty.

to die for

During the first half of the twentieth century, segregation was a huge problem in the United States. African American women could not buy hair products from the same stores as white women. Madam C. J. Walker got around this by selling her products door-to-door in black neighborhoods. Her best-selling products included coconut-oil shampoo and Glossine, a pressing oil to straighten and smooth the hair.

SHORT IS -BEAUTIFUL-

Life changed dramatically after World War I ended in 1918. Short hair came into style for both men and women as the modern age really began.

During World War I (1914–1918), the U.S. Navy introduced compulsory haircuts for all sailors. Before long, all the other branches of the military had followed suit.

OFF WITH YOUR HAIR

The rules were very strict: the hair on the top of the head could be no more than 1 inch long (2.5 cm). That was short! After the war, the rules were relaxed to allow a whole 2 inches (5 cm). U.S. forces were popular heroes after their victory in the war, so when they returned to the United States, other men copied their short haircuts. New styling products for men, such as Brylcreem, let men slick back their cropped hair to copy the stars of the silent screen.

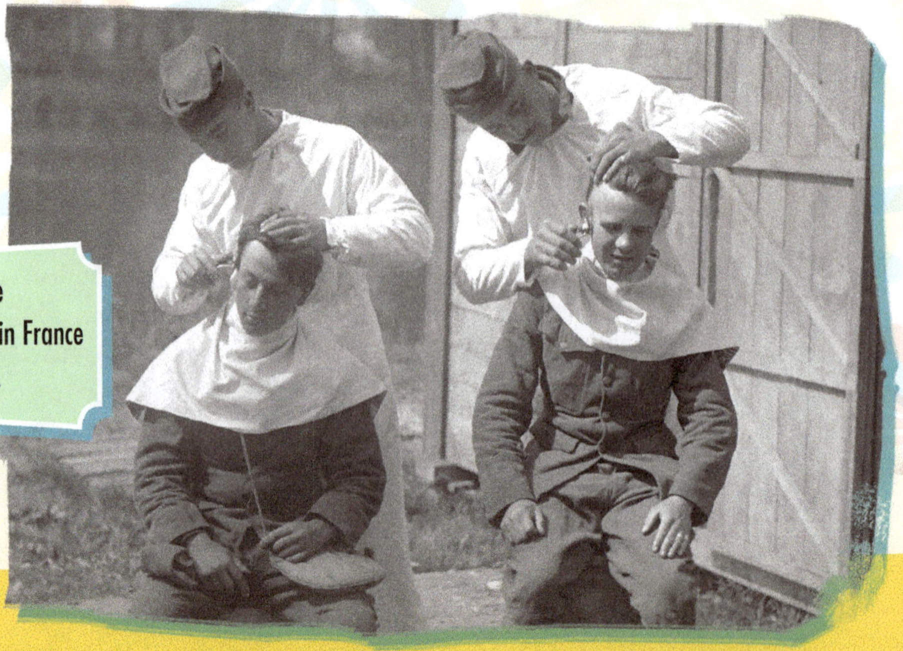

U.S. soldiers receive regulation haircuts in France during World War I.

IN A FLAP

Queen Victoria died in 1901. Her death marked the beginning of the end for long hair hidden away under bonnets. World War I brought more change, as many women worked and earned their own money for the first time. Their new freedom brought new attitudes. Daring young women chopped their hair short into the fashionable "**bob**" cut worn by movie stars such as Louise Brooks, known as the It Girls. The number of hair salons jumped from 5,000 to 23,000 to keep up with demand for the new short look, cut straight around the head. Curls were optional. The young women who led the way, called **flappers**, wore makeup and fashionable straight, short dresses.

Brylcreem, introduced in 1928, is a mixture of water, oil, and beeswax.

hello beautiful

Clara Bow became the original "It Girl" when she starred in the 1927 movie *It*. She was the most famous silent movie star to survive the introduction of the "talkies." With her short, curly, bobbed dark hair, Bow helped set the trend for the daring, independent young women known as the flappers.

Clara Bow's distinctive hair made her a movie idol in the late 1920s.

PILES OF -HAIR-

The 1950s saw a return to big hair thanks to new products that made hair easier to style. Soon women everywhere were sporting the look.

Jackie Kennedy was a fashion icon both during her time in the White House and afterward.

In the 1950s a new product found its way into the homes of millions of women: hair spray! The spray can had been developed during World War II. It was mainly used for insect killers. Now cosmetic companies used it to package a sticky, resin-based spray that kept hair from blowing around.

ALL PUFFED UP

Hair spray allowed hairstylists and women at home to create all kinds of new looks. One popular early look was the bouffant. It was made famous in the early 1960s by the glamorous First Lady Jackie Kennedy, wife of President John F. Kennedy. The bouffant was a puffed-out pageboy style created by winding hair in large rollers, allowing it to dry, and then drowning it in hairspray. The bouffant led the way for all kinds of other puffed-up hair.

BUSY AS A BEE

Hair spray allowed women to comb their hair and then tease it into high mounds. The new styles were heaven for any woman who worried about having thin hair. Those who could not get the look with their own hair wore a hairpiece or a bouffant wig. The tallest style was the beehive, which appeared around 1958 and remained a hit into the 1960s. It needed a lot of hair spray to get enough height. It was sometimes called a B-52 after a large bomber, because its shape resembled the aircraft's nose!

The beehive got its name from its resemblance to the conical shape of old-fashioned beehives.

hello beautiful

Some of the biggest music stars of the 1960s wore beehives, including the soul singer Aretha Franklin and girl band the Ronettes. Some performers still wear beehives, including the singers Beyoncé and Adele. Today, the most famous beehive possibly belongs to Marge Simpson from the TV series *The Simpsons*. Once thought old-fashioned, the beehive is back with a bang!

HAIR
- TRIBES -

In the second half of the twentieth century, hair became tribal. Short, long, or shaved hair were signs of people's ideas and loyalties.

The movement started in the mid-1960s, when the British pop group The Beatles caused a scandal by growing their hair over their collars. Their fans called them the Mop Tops, and copied the haircut around the world.

HIPPIES AND AFROS

The hippie movement emerged in San Francisco a few years later. Hippies wanted to let their hair down—literally! Both men and women grew their hair long and never styled it, apart from putting flowers in it or wrapping **bandannas** around their heads. Meanwhile, African Americans also let their hair grow naturally as the Afro became popular. The performers Jimi Hendrix and James Brown both sported long Afros.

Students were sent home from some schools when they had haircuts like the Beatles.

THE SEVENTIES AND ON

The punk movement that started in the United States and England in the late 1970s introduced some of the most shocking hairstyles in history. Punks dyed their hair purple, green, blue, or any other color that didn't look natural. Some shaved part of their heads, leaving a central strip of long hair that was gelled into an upright spike, known as a mohawk. Men and women both did this. Other people shaved their heads completely. Some thought this gave off an aggressive look.

The punk mohawk was said to be inspired by the haircuts of some Native Americans in the nineteenth century.

hello beautiful

In the late 1960s and early 1970s, the African American actress Marsha Hunt was as famous for her striking Afro hairstyle as for her acting skills. Although she only had two lines to speak in the rock musical *Hair*, which played to full houses every night in London in 1968, Hunt grabbed the press headlines because of her striking look.

Chapter 6
THE TWENTY-FIRST - CENTURY -

Today, hair has never been more free, but in some ways, it is still restricted. Religion and culture still play an important part in how we wear our hair.

Today, hair fashions come and go. Hair can be long or short, styled or unstyled, dyed or natural. Movie stars, TV celebrities, and even princesses still have an influence on the trends—but there is one significant difference in how we learn about new hairstyles.

A young woman records a hairstyling vlog as she shapes her hair with curling tongs.

ANYTHING GOES

Thanks to blogs and vlogs, the Internet has become the go-to hair sourcebook of choice for millions of young people. Videos on creating a whole range of styles are widely available, as are reviews of hair products. It has never been so easy to buy natural or organic hair products. Some hair dyes still use chemicals—although not the poisonous leads and sulfates of the past—but plant-based dyes like those our ancestors made are back in fashion. They include chamomile flowers to enhance blonde hair or henna to dye hair red.

RESTRICTIONS APPLY

Today, some women of certain faiths still keep their hair covered for religious reasons. Even though the rule is not explicitly stated in the Islamic holy book, the Quran, many women who follow certain branches of the Islamic faith still choose to cover their hair. Muslim women may wear coverings ranging from hijabs that cover their head to burkas that cover their heads and faces. Some **orthodox** Jewish women shave their heads upon marriage and then wear a wig.

In the Christian world, many women wear a veil on their wedding day. Women who visit the Vatican in Rome to meet the pope traditionally had to cover their heads with a black veil. Pope Francis, who became head of the Roman Catholic Church in 2013, has relaxed the dress code.

The market in hair and beauty products will be worth $16 billion by 2020.

Many Muslim women cover their hair in public with a traditional covering called a hijab.

FUN
- TIME -

Whether it is real or artificial, fake hair is back in fashion. It's a throwback to ancient hair care!

Thousands of years ago, the ancient Egyptians wore black or colored wigs over their shaved heads and were not concerned if they did not look real. Today, the fake wig is back!

PAST FUTURE

Fun wigs do not pretend to look real. They are made from shiny nylon and come in all kinds of colors not associated with real hair. Think pink, blue, orange, and green. Similar wigs have been popular before, such as for masked balls in sixteenth-century Venice.

Many modern wigs are made in colors that no one could possibly mistake for real hair.

IT'S REAL!

Another twenty-first-century trend that has been around for millennia is wearing other people's hair. Throughout history, women have made wigs from real hair. Roman women cut their slaves' hair to make extensions. Later, in colonial times, Indian and Brazilian women sold their hair to make money. Today, buying real human hair is big business. Fair hair costs three times more than dark hair, because it is in shorter supply. Hair extensions made from real human hair are now so well made that it is almost impossible to tell who is wearing hair extensions and who is not.

A store displays a range of luxury wigs made from real human hair.

to die for

The Japanese lead the way in wearing fake colored wigs to copy their favorite characters from movies, books, online games, and manga comics. The hobby is known as cosplay, an abbreviation of "costume play." Fans have a choice of more than 100 different colors for wigs that range from helmet shapes to Afro styles.

People around the world use wigs as part of costumes when they dress up as fantasy characters.

-TIMELINE-

c. 1500 BC	The Assyrians conquer Babylon, introducing their tightly curled hairstyles and beards.
478 BC	Hatshepsut comes to the throne in Egypt. As pharaoh, she wears a false beard.
c. 600 BC	The chignon is a popular hairstyle in Athens in ancient Greece.
146 BC	Rome conquers Greece, and Romans adopt Greek hairstyles.
c. AD 1	The Roman emperor Julius Caesar begins wearing a laurel crown to hide his baldness.
AD 303	The first barbershop opens in Rome.
AD 634	Women start covering their heads in some Muslim countries.
1073	Pope Gregory forbids monks to wear beards. The clean-shaven look soon spreads to men throughout society.
1429	Joan of Arc leads French soldiers into battle against the English at Orléans with her distinctive pageboy haircut.
1558	Queen Elizabeth I comes to the English throne. She begins a fashion for red hair.
1649	Before being beheaded during the English Civil War, King Charles I asks the executioner, "Is my hair well?"
1685	The fontange becomes the most popular hairstyle for women.
c. 1780	Hairstyles up to 3 feet (0.9 m) tall become popular in France. The hair soon becomes home to vermin.

c. 1785	Beau Brummell becomes leader of the dandies in London. He is said to use three hairdressers at once.
1789	After the French Revolution, the wigs worn by kings and nobles go out of fashion in France.
1798	A tax on wig powder leads to the decline of wigs in Britain.
1804	Josephine becomes empress of France. She leads a reintroduction of hairstyles based on those of ancient Greece.
1837	Victoria becomes queen of Britain. She influences modest, natural styles in which the hair is covered with a bonnet.
1854	British soldiers in the Crimean War grow full beards to help keep their faces warm in winter.
1872	Marcel Grateau invents the Marcel wave, later the basis of the permanent wave, or perm.
1905	Sarah Breedlove dreams of a recipe for hair cream. Trading as Madam C. J. Walker, she becomes one of the first American female millionaires.
1918	At the end of World War I, men and women begin to wear their hair short in an echo of military styles during the conflict.
1920s	Young American women known as flappers wear makeup and have their hair cut short.
1950s	The invention of hairspray enables women to pile their hair into "big" styles such as the beehive.
1968	U.S. actress Marsha Hunt causes a sensation on the stage with her Afro hairstyle.
1977	Punks appear in the United States and Britain, with colored, spiked hair.
1984	The word "cosplay" is coined to describe dressing up as fantasy characters, complete with wigs.
2006	Vloggers, sometimes known as beauty YouTubers, begin broadcasting videos about hair and makeup on the Internet.

-GLOSSARY-

Afro a hairstyle of tight curls sticking out all around the head
auburn a reddish-brown color
bandannas large handkerchiefs worn around the neck or head
Black Pride a political movement to celebrate African American culture
bob a style in which hair is cut evenly short, above the shoulders
bohemian socially unconventional
bonnet a hat tied under the chin with a brim framing the face
bouffant hair styled to stand out from the head in a rounded shape
braids lengths of hair woven from three or more strands
caustic soda a chemical used to make soap and other cleaners
chignon a knot or coil of hair at the back of the head
courtiers people at a royal court
dandy a man who pays excessive attention to his appearance
flappers fashionable young women in the 1920s who broke the rules of accepted behavior and appearance
grunge a style of rock music from the 1990s
hair extensions lengths of false hair woven into someone's real hair
immoral having poor standards of behavior
laurel a shrub with dark, glossy leaves
leeches bloodsucking worms
macassar oil an oily preparation used to make hair slick and glossy
minerals natural substances, such as crystals and salts
modesty the quality of not calling attention to oneself
nobility an elite, privileged class at the top of society
orthodox following the strict rules of a religion
pageboy cut a shoulder-length haircut with the ends curled under
pharaohs rulers of ancient Egypt
plaits lengths of braided hair
platinum a silvery-white color
potash a substance made from wood ash
quince a pear-shaped Asian fruit
resin a sticky substance released from the bark of some trees
Romantic an artistic movement based on strong emotions
saffron an orange-yellow coloring made from crocus flowers
starch a powder made from plants used as a stiffener
symmetrical cut a hairstyle in which both sides echo each other exactly
toxic poisonous
vain having excessive pride in one's own appearance
veil a piece of fine material worn by women to cover their hair and face
vermin harmful worms or insects

-FOR MORE INFORMATION-

BOOKS

Baum, Margaux. *Fashion and Clothing*. New York, NY: Rosen Publishing, 2017.

Ehrmann, Johanna. *The Life of a Colonial Wigmaker.* New York, NY: PowerKids Press, 2014.

Krull, Kathleen. *Big Wig: A Little History of Hair.* New York, NY: Arthur A. Levine Books, 2011.

McKissack, Patricia and Frederick. *Madam C. J. Walker: Inventor and Millionaire.* Berkeley Heights, NJ: Enslow Publishers, 2013.

WEBSITES

Annie Turnbo Malone
www.encyclopedia.com/people/history/historians-miscellaneous-biographies/annie-turnbo-malone
This webpage features a biography of the inventor Annie Turnbo Malone.

Clothing and Hair Styles
rome.mrdonn.org/clothing.html
This page includes lots of facts about early Roman hair and clothing trends.

10 Fun Facts about Ancient Egyptian Wigs
www.egyptabout.com/2016/11/ancient-egyptian-wigs.html
This article is all about the wigs worn in ancient Egypt.

-INDEX-